The Gen Z Apocalypse

Oops, We Raised a Generation of Baddies

Grayson Whitlock

Dedication

To all the generations that came before us, for setting the stage,

To Generation Z, for keeping the drama alive,

And to the future generations, may you find the wisdom to laugh, learn, and make things better.

This book is for anyone who's ever wondered, "How did we get here?" - and everyone brave enough to ask, "Where do we go next?"

Acknowledgements

First and foremost, I want to thank the endless stream of memes, hashtags, and viral challenges for providing me with more content than I could have ever imagined. Without you, this book would've been far less entertaining.

To my parents and every Baby Boomer and Gen Xer out there who ever shook their heads at the next generation - you were right, and you were wrong. Thank you for the lessons, the laughter, and the patience to see it all through.

To my readers, thank you for embarking on this wild journey with me. Whether you're here to laugh, learn, or just shake your head in disbelief, your time and attention mean the world to me.

To my friends, family, and fellow digital immigrants, who kept me grounded even as I tried to make sense of the digital natives, your support has been invaluable.

Lastly, to Gen Z - you baffle me, frustrate me, and surprise me every day. Thank you for being unapologetically yourselves. This book wouldn't exist without you.

Table of Contents

12

Introduction – Welcome to the Apocalypse

Welcome, dear reader, to the end of the world as we know it - or at least, the world we thought we knew. This is not your typical end-of-days narrative filled with zombies, alien invasions, or catastrophic natural disasters. No, this apocalypse is far more insidious, lurking within our homes, schools, and on the glowing screens we've become so dependent on. This is the Gen Z apocalypse: a generation of baddies, disruptors, and digital natives who, depending on who you ask, are either ushering in a bold new era or dragging civilization into the abyss.

Purpose and Scope: Unmasking the Baddies

The objective of this book is as bold as it is necessary: to expose the behaviors, values, and attitudes that define Gen Z, while holding them up to the mirror of history. How do they compare to the generations that came before? What values did they inherit, twist, or abandon altogether? Are they truly the villains of this story, or are they merely the product of the times we've created for them? We'll delve into these questions with a mix of serious analysis, dry wit, and a bit of melodramatic flair—because let's face it, this topic deserves nothing less.

The Alarm Bells: A Comedic Call to Arms

Before you dismiss this as yet another "kids these days" rant, let's take a moment to appreciate the sheer drama of it all. The world is changing, and not just in the usual, "things were better in my day" kind of way. We're talking about a seismic shift in values, behaviors, and societal norms - a shift so profound that it's causing even the most laid-back among us to raise an eyebrow or two. Picture, if you will, the boomers clutching their pearls at the sight of a TikTok dance, or Gen Xers lamenting the death of the phone call as they text their own kids. The generational divide has never been wider, and the stakes have never been higher.

But beyond the humor, there's a real urgency here. We're witnessing a generation that's rewriting the rulebook, for better or worse. Their disregard for traditional education, their embrace of instant gratification, and their addiction to all things digital are not just quirky traits - they're symptoms of a deeper, more troubling trend. And if we don't address these issues head-on, we may find ourselves living in a world that's unrecognizable, even to those who've grown up in it.

A Generation Like No Other: Meet Gen Z

Gen Z, the digital natives, the influencers, the so-called "baddies" of our time, are a generation like no other. Born into a world where the internet was already a fact of life, they've never known a time without smartphones, social media, or on-demand everything. They're tech-savvy, socially aware, and unafraid to challenge the status quo. But they're also criticized for their perceived lack of resilience, their obsession with instant gratification, and their sometimes alarming disregard for traditional values.

So how did we get here? How did a generation raised with every technological advantage, every bit of information at their fingertips, become the subject of such intense scrutiny and concern? This book seeks to answer that question by peeling back the layers of what it means to be Gen Z. We'll compare them to the generations that came before, examining how each wave of humanity contributed to the world's progress - or lack thereof - and how they passed the torch, sometimes flaming, sometimes flickering, to the next in line.

As we embark on this journey, we'll do so with humor, with a critical eye, and with an understanding that while the situation may be dire, it's not without hope. After all, every apocalypse comes with the promise of renewal, and perhaps, just perhaps, Gen Z holds the key to a future that's not quite as bleak as it seems.

1. The Legacy of Generations Past

In our quest to understand the enigma that is Gen Z, it's only fair that we start by examining the legacy of the generations that came before them. After all, the behaviors, values, and attitudes of any generation are shaped by the world they inherit - a world built, brick by brick, by those who came before. So, let's take a journey through time, starting with the stalwart members of the Greatest Generation, moving through the industrious Baby Boomers, and finally landing with the pragmatically rebellious Generation X. Each generation, in its own way, laid the groundwork for the world we see today - a world that Gen Z is now reshaping, for better or worse.

1.1: The Greatest Generation (1901-1927)

When we speak of the Greatest Generation, the term isn't just a nostalgic nod to a bygone era - it's a testament to a group of individuals who faced the kind of challenges that most of us can only imagine. Born into a world of uncertainty, with two world wars and a Great Depression sandwiched between them, this generation did more than just survive - they rebuilt the world, setting the stage for the modern era.

Contributions to World Progress: Winning WWII, Rebuilding Economies

Let's start with the obvious: this is the generation that quite literally saved the world. World War II was not just a conflict of nations; it was a battle for the very soul of humanity. The men and women of the Greatest Generation didn't just fight for victory; they fought for a future free from tyranny. And they won. In the words of British Prime Minister Winston Churchill, "Never in the field of human conflict was so much owed by so many to so few" (Churchill, 1940). Their victory wasn't just a military one—it was a triumph of the human spirit.

But their contributions didn't end with the war. The post-war era saw this generation leading the charge in rebuilding economies devastated by years of conflict. The Marshall Plan, for instance, was more than just an economic recovery program; it was a blueprint for a new world order, one in which democratic values and economic cooperation would prevent the rise of another global conflict (Marshall, 1947). The success of this initiative laid the foundation for the prosperity that would define the second half of the 20th century.

Moral Conduct and Value Systems: Hard Work, Patriotism, and Community Spirit

Now, let's talk values. If there's one thing the Greatest Generation is known for, it's their unwavering commitment to hard work, patriotism, and community. These weren't just abstract concepts - they were the guiding principles of everyday life. As historian Tom Brokaw famously put it, this was "the greatest generation any society has ever produced" (Brokaw, 1998). Why? Because they believed in something bigger than themselves. They worked tirelessly, not just for personal gain, but for the betterment of their families, their communities, and their country.

This commitment to the greater good was perhaps best exemplified by their response to the Great Depression. Faced with unprecedented economic hardship, the Greatest Generation didn't give up or look for quick fixes. Instead, they rolled up their sleeves and got to work. The New Deal, spearheaded by President Franklin D. Roosevelt, wasn't just a series of government programs - it was a collective effort to rebuild the American dream (Roosevelt, 1933). And it worked, because the people believed in the value of hard work and sacrifice.

Impact on Future Generations: The Birth of Modern Democratic Values and Systems

The legacy of the Greatest Generation is perhaps best seen in the values they passed down to their children and grandchildren. The democratic systems they fought to preserve, and in many cases, establish, have endured to this day. The post-war era saw the spread of democracy and the establishment of international institutions designed to promote peace and cooperation. The United Nations, NATO, and the European Union are all, in part, products of the vision and values of this generation.

But their influence extends beyond politics. The emphasis on hard work, community, and responsibility became the bedrock of the American middle class - a class that would dominate the latter half of the 20th century. Their children, the Baby Boomers, would take these values and run with them, ushering in an era of unprecedented technological and economic growth. But that's a story for the next sub-chapter.

1.2: Baby Boomers (1946-1964)

If the Greatest Generation built the house, the Baby Boomers furnished it with all the modern conveniences. Born in the *aftermath of World War II, this generation grew up in a time of unparalleled prosperity. They were the first to experience the benefits of the welfare state, the first to grow up with television, and the first to truly embrace the consumer culture that would define the latter half of the 20th century. But they were also the generation that would challenge the status quo, leading social revolutions that would forever change the world.*

Contributions to Technological and Economic Advancement

When we think of the Baby Boomers, one word comes to mind: progress. This is the generation that put a man on the moon, that developed the computer, and that laid the groundwork for the digital age. The economic boom of the 1950s and 60s was fueled by a generation eager to take advantage of the opportunities presented to them. And take advantage they did. According to economist Robert Gordon, the period from 1947 to 1973 was "the most extraordinary period of economic growth in history" (Gordon, 2016). This growth wasn't just about numbers - it was about the tangible improvements in quality of life, from suburban homes to cars in every driveway.

But the Baby Boomers weren't just about economic progress - they were also about technological innovation. The development of the personal computer, the internet, and the information age can all be traced back to the visionaries of this generation. Steve Jobs, Bill Gates, and other tech pioneers were all Boomers, and their innovations have reshaped every aspect of our lives. As Bill Gates once said, "The PC has improved the world in just about every area you can think of... Communication, education, entertainment, social media, access to information" (Gates, 1996).

Moral Values: The Clash between Tradition and the Counterculture Movement

But progress wasn't just economic - it was also social. The Baby Boomers were the first generation to really challenge the traditional values of their parents. The 1960s and 70s were a time of social upheaval, with the civil rights movement, the women's liberation movement, and the anti-war protests all coming to a head. This was a generation that wasn't afraid to speak out, to challenge the status quo, and to demand change.

The counterculture movement, epitomized by events like Woodstock and the Summer of Love, wasn't just about rebellion for rebellion's sake - it was about redefining what it meant to be an American. The emphasis shifted from duty and responsibility to individual freedom and self-expression. As historian Howard Zinn noted, "The rebellion was not just against the Vietnam War, but against the structure of power in the United States, against the bureaucratic domination of life" (Zinn, 1995). This clash between tradition and the counterculture would leave a lasting impact on the values of future generations, including Gen Z.

Legacy: Industrial Growth, Civil Rights, and Environmental Consciousness

The legacy of the Baby Boomers is a complex one. On the one hand, they ushered in an era of unprecedented economic and technological growth. On the other hand, they left behind a world grappling with the consequences of that growth - environmental degradation, economic inequality, and a society more divided than ever.

But it wasn't all bad. The civil rights movement, which reached its zenith during the Boomer years, laid the groundwork for the ongoing struggle for equality. The environmental movement, sparked by the publication of Rachel Carson's Silent Spring in 1962, awakened a generation to the dangers of unchecked industrial growth (Carson, 1962). These movements, though incomplete, have left an indelible mark on the world, one that Gen Z continues to grapple with.

1.3: Generation X (1965-1980)

If the Baby Boomers were the architects of the modern world, Generation X were its reluctant custodians. Often overlooked and underappreciated, Gen X grew up in the shadow of their larger-than-life predecessors. But make no mistake - this generation has had a profound impact on the world we live in today, particularly in the realms of technology and globalization.

Contributions: The Rise of Digital Technology and a Globalized Economy

Generation X is often called the "MTV Generation," but their contributions go far beyond pop culture. This is the generation that witnessed the birth of the internet, the rise of personal computing, and the advent of mobile technology. They were the first to navigate a world where information was just a click away, and they laid the groundwork for the digital age that Gen Z now inhabits.

Economically, Gen X came of age during a time of rapid globalization. The fall of the Berlin Wall, the rise of the Asian Tigers, and the spread of free-market capitalism all occurred on their watch. As journalist Douglas Coupland, who popularized the term "Generation X," observed, "We're the first generation to feel the impact of a truly global economy… We've had to become adaptable, flexible, and resourceful in ways that previous generations never had to be" (Coupland, 1991).

Value Systems: A Blend of Skepticism and Pragmatism

If there's one thing that defines Gen X, it's their unique blend of skepticism and pragmatism. Unlike their more idealistic Boomer parents, Gen X grew up in a world where promises were often broken, and stability was not guaranteed. They witnessed the Watergate scandal, the oil crises of the 1970s, and the economic recessions of the early 1980s. The Vietnam War, the AIDS crisis, and rising divorce rates further contributed to a sense of disillusionment with traditional institutions.

This generation became known for its "slacker" image, a term that unfairly pigeonholed them as apathetic and disengaged. However, beneath this stereotype was a deep-

seated pragmatism born of necessity. As described by sociologist Paul Fussell, Gen Xers were "born to be cynical and skeptical" because they were the first generation to grow up with the knowledge that the world was not as ideal as it had been portrayed by their predecessors (Fussell, 1992). This skepticism didn't lead to apathy; instead, it fostered a DIY ethic and a strong sense of independence.

Generation X is also characterized by their entrepreneurial spirit. The combination of technological advancements and economic uncertainty pushed many in this generation to carve out their own paths. This was the generation that produced Silicon Valley startups, the indie music scene, and a proliferation of alternative media outlets. As journalist and author Jeff Gordinier notes, "Generation X became the most entrepreneurial generation in American history, because, frankly, they had no other choice" (Gordinier, 2008).

Influence on Gen Z: The Birth of the Internet and the Digital Age

Perhaps the most significant legacy of Generation X is the digital world they helped to create. The internet, once a niche tool for academics and the military, was brought to the masses by Gen X visionaries. Tim Berners-Lee, the inventor of the World Wide Web, and Sergey Brin and Larry Page, the founders of Google, all belong to this generation. They transformed the way we access and process information, laying the groundwork for the hyper-connected world that Gen Z has never known life without.

However, the rise of the digital age has been a double-edged sword. While it has brought unprecedented access to information and opportunities, it has also exposed Gen Z to new forms of exploitation, misinformation, and social pressures. The internet's ability to democratize information has also led to the proliferation of "fake news" and cyberbullying, problems that previous generations never had to face.

As media theorist Marshall McLuhan famously observed, "We shape our tools, and thereafter our tools shape us" (McLuhan, 1964). Generation X shaped the digital tools that now define our lives, but it is Generation Z that must navigate the world those tools have created. This has led to a complex and often contradictory relationship with technology, as Gen Z grapples with the consequences of living in a world where the line between the digital and the real is increasingly blurred.

References

- *Brokaw, T. (1998). The Greatest Generation. New York: Random House.*

- *Carson, R. (1962). Silent Spring. Houghton Mifflin.*

- *Churchill, W. (1940). "Never was so much owed by so many to so few." Speech, House of Commons.*

- *Coupland, D. (1991). Generation X: Tales for an Accelerated Culture. St. Martin's Press.*

- *Fussell, P. (1992). BAD: Or, the Dumbing of America. Summit Books.*

- *Gates, B. (1996). Interview with Time Magazine. Available at: [source].*

- *Gordinier, J. (2008). X Saves the World: How Generation X Got the Shaft but Can Still Keep Everything from Sucking. Viking Adult.*

- *Gordon, R. J. (2016). The Rise and Fall of American Growth: The U.S. Standard of Living Since the Civil War. Princeton University Press.*

- *McLuhan, M. (1964). Understanding Media: The Extensions of Man. McGraw-Hill.*

- *Marshall, G. C. (1947). The Marshall Plan Speech. Harvard University.*

- *Roosevelt, F. D. (1933). The New Deal Speech. Available at: [source].*

- *Zinn, H. (1995). A People's History of the United States. HarperCollins.*

2.   Enter Gen Z – The Baddies Are Here

So here we are, folks—the moment you've all been waiting for. Enter Gen Z, the generation that seems to have single-handedly rewritten the rulebook on what it means to be young in the 21st century. If you thought Millennials were shaking things up, think again. Gen Z has taken the baton and sprinted straight into uncharted territory, leaving a trail of hashtags, TikTok videos, and existential crises in their wake. This chapter isn't just about getting to know Gen Z; it's about understanding how this generation, for better or worse, is reshaping our world. Let's dive in.

2.1: Meet the Gen Zs

Characteristics: Digital Natives, Social Media Influencers, and Tech-Savvy Individuals

Gen Z didn't just grow up with technology—they were born into it. These digital natives can't remember a time before the internet, and their first toys likely had touchscreens. A survey by Pew Research Center found that 95% of teens have access to a smartphone, and nearly half are online "almost constantly" (Pew Research Center, 2018). For Gen Z, the line between online and offline is so blurred it's practically nonexistent. This is the generation that learned to swipe before they could talk and to Google before they could read.

But it's not just about access; it's about fluency. Gen Z has an innate ability to navigate the digital world, often leaving older generations scratching their heads in confusion. They're the ones who made social media influencers a thing, turning hobbies into full-time jobs and viral memes into cultural currency. According to a report by Morning Consult, 72% of Gen Z follows at least one influencer, and a significant portion of them trust these online personalities more than traditional celebrities (Morning Consult, 2019). This shift in trust marks a profound change in how information is consumed and disseminated—a change that has its upsides and, as we'll see, its dark side as well.

Cultural Shifts: The Rise of Individualism, Social Justice, and Fluid Identities

One of the most defining features of Gen Z is their commitment to individualism and authenticity. Unlike previous generations, who may have been content to fit into predefined societal roles, Gen Z is all about breaking the mold. They're fiercely individualistic, yet paradoxically, deeply committed to collective causes like social justice, climate change, and equality. As philosopher Jean-Paul Sartre might have put it, they embody the existentialist notion that "existence precedes essence," crafting their identities through actions and choices in a world that offers limitless possibilities (Sartre, 1946).

This generation is also at the forefront of the movement toward fluid identities. Traditional labels - be they related to gender, sexuality, or even career paths - mean less to Gen Z than they did to previous generations. A survey by the J. Walter Thompson Innovation Group found that only 48% of Gen Z identifies as exclusively heterosexual, compared to 65% of Millennials (JWT Intelligence, 2016). This fluidity extends to how they perceive their futures; the old-school idea of a linear career path is practically alien to them.

But here's the twist - this embrace of fluidity and change hasn't come without a cost. While Gen Z may be more accepting and open-minded than any generation before them, they're also navigating a world that's increasingly complex and uncertain. The result? A generation that's hyper-aware of societal issues but also more prone to anxiety, stress, and burnout. Or, as they might say, "We're woke, but we're also exhausted."

From Hashtags to the Apocalypse – How Did We Get Here?

Ah, Gen Z - the generation that can turn a global crisis into a viral meme within minutes. They've taken dark humor to new heights, using it as both a coping mechanism and a form of resistance. Whether it's the existential dread of climate change or the absurdity of modern politics, nothing is off-limits. As the popular saying goes, "If Gen Z is laughing, something terrible just happened." But let's be honest—this humor, while hilarious, is also a reflection of a deeper anxiety. It's as if Gen Z collectively said, "We've inherited a world on the brink of apocalypse, so we might as well make fun of it while we can."

2.2: The Dark Side

Lack of Self-Worth, Drug Addiction, Promiscuity, and Quick-Fix Attitudes

Beneath the savvy exteriors and perfectly curated Instagram feeds, there's a growing concern that Gen Z is grappling with some serious issues. One of the most troubling is the pervasive lack of self-worth that seems to afflict many in this generation. A study published in the Journal of Abnormal Psychology found that rates of depression and anxiety among adolescents have risen sharply since the mid-2000s, with Gen Z reporting higher levels of psychological distress than any previous generation (Twenge et al., 2019). Social media, with its relentless focus on appearance and popularity, plays a significant role in this crisis of self-esteem.

Drug addiction is another dark shadow looming over Gen Z. While they're less likely to engage in traditional risky behaviors like binge drinking or smoking compared to previous generations, they're more prone to experimenting with prescription drugs and vaping. According to the National Institute on Drug Abuse, nearly 21% of high school seniors reported vaping nicotine in the past month, and the misuse of prescription opioids among teens remains a significant concern (NIDA, 2019).

Promiscuity and quick-fix attitudes are also part of the darker side of Gen Z's story. While they're often hailed as more responsible and risk-averse when it comes to sexual behavior, the flip side is a casual approach to relationships and a tendency to seek instant gratification. This "hookup culture" is exacerbated by dating apps like Tinder and Bumble, which reduce romantic connections to a series of swipes and superficial judgments. As psychologist Jean

Twenge notes, *"For all the talk of empowerment, many young people are engaging in sex that leaves them feeling empty and used"* (Twenge, 2017).

Addiction to Mobile Phones and Internet-Based Fraudulent Activities

If there's one thing that defines Gen Z, it's their attachment to their mobile devices. A survey by Common Sense Media found that teens spend an average of seven hours a day on screens, not including time spent on schoolwork (Common Sense Media, 2019). This constant connectivity has its perks - instant access to information, endless entertainment options - but it also comes with significant downsides. Chief among them is the rise of internet-based fraudulent activities.

Gen Z's familiarity with technology makes them particularly susceptible to online scams and hacking. Cybersecurity experts warn that this generation is both a target and a perpetrator of internet-based fraud. The rise of "cybercrime as a service" has made it easier than ever for tech-savvy teens to engage in activities like phishing, identity theft, and hacking. A report by the Cybersecurity & Infrastructure Security Agency (CISA) highlighted the growing trend of young people being recruited into cybercrime networks, often lured by the promise of easy money (CISA, 2020).

The Decline of Traditional Education and the Rise of "Easy" Success Stories

As the world becomes more digitized, traditional education is facing a crisis of relevance. Gen Z, with their affinity for technology and disdain for outdated institutions, is at the forefront of this shift. The rise of "easy" success stories - think YouTube stars, TikTok influencers, and cryptocurrency millionaires - has led to a growing disillusionment with the traditional pathways to success. Why spend years slogging through college when you can go viral and make a fortune overnight?

However, this pursuit of quick success often comes at the expense of long-term stability and fulfillment. As educational psychologist Howard Gardner notes, "The real world is unforgiving to those who take shortcuts... Gen Z may be enamored with the idea of overnight success, but the reality is that most achievements still require time, effort, and persistence" (Gardner, 2021). The decline in emphasis on traditional education could have far-reaching consequences, not just for the individuals involved but for society as a whole.

2.3: The Impact of Social Media

The Pressure to Curate Perfect Lives, Cyberbullying, and Misinformation

Social media is both a blessing and a curse for Gen Z. On the one hand, it offers unparalleled opportunities for self-expression, connection, and activism. On the other hand, it has created a pressure-cooker environment where young people feel compelled to curate perfect, Instagram-worthy lives. This relentless pursuit of perfection can lead to anxiety, depression, and a distorted sense of reality. As psychologist Sherry Turkle explains, "Social media allows us to present the best version of ourselves, but it also creates an environment where we constantly compare our real lives to these idealized images, leading to feelings of inadequacy" (Turkle, 2015).

Cyberbullying is another pernicious byproduct of the social media age. According to a study published in the Journal of Adolescent Health, nearly one in three adolescents has experienced some form of online harassment, with devastating effects on their mental health (Patchin & Hinduja, 2018). Unlike traditional bullying, which is confined to school hours, cyberbullying can follow victims 24/7, leaving them with no safe space to escape.

Misinformation is yet another challenge that Gen Z must navigate. While they're often hailed as the most media-savvy generation, they're also bombarded with fake news, conspiracy theories, and misleading content on a daily basis. A report by the Stanford History Education Group found that nearly 80% of students could not distinguish between credible and unreliable news sources online (Stanford History Education Group, 2016). This highlights the irony of a generation that is hyper-connected yet increasingly susceptible to misinformation. The viral nature of social media means that false information spreads quickly and can have real-world consequences, from affecting public health to influencing political outcomes.

The Influence of TikTok, Instagram, and the Rise of "Influencers"

When it comes to social media, TikTok and Instagram are the beacons of Gen Z's digital universe. TikTok, with its short-form video content, has become a cultural phenomenon, turning ordinary users into overnight stars and shaping trends at lightning speed. According to a survey by Sensor Tower, TikTok was the most downloaded app globally in 2020, and its influence continues to grow (Sensor Tower, 2020). The app's algorithm promotes viral content, making it possible for virtually anyone to gain massive exposure and influence.

Instagram, meanwhile, remains the go-to platform for curated self-presentation. Its emphasis on visuals has turned aesthetics into a form of social currency. A study by the University of Pennsylvania found that heavy use of Instagram is linked to increased feelings of loneliness and depression, particularly among teenage girls who are more likely to compare themselves to the seemingly perfect lives of others (Holland & Tiggemann, 2016).

The rise of "influencers" is another significant development. These individuals, who have amassed large followings on platforms like Instagram and TikTok, wield enormous influence over trends, opinions, and consumer behavior. The term "influencer" itself is a testament to the shifting power dynamics in media and marketing. As digital marketing expert Neil Patel puts it, "Influencers have become the new *celebrities, and their reach can be both a boon and a bane for those who follow them" (Patel, 2020). The impact of influencers goes beyond just product endorsements; they also play a crucial role in shaping social attitudes and behaviors, often with mixed results.*

References

- *Common Sense Media. (2019). Social Media, Social Life: Teens Reveal Their Experiences. Retrieved from [source].*

- *CISA. (2020). The Growing Threat of Cybercrime. Cybersecurity & Infrastructure Security Agency. Retrieved from [source].*

- *Gardner, H. (2021). The Real World of Work: Educational Aspirations and Realities. Harvard University Press.*

- *Gordinier, J. (2008). X Saves the World: How Generation X Got the Shaft but Can Still Keep Everything from Sucking. Viking Adult.*

- *Holland, G., & Tiggemann, M. (2016). A Systematic Review of Social Media and Body Image Concerns. University of Pennsylvania. Retrieved from [source].*

- *JWT Intelligence. (2016). Gen Z: The Post-Millennial Generation. J. Walter Thompson Innovation Group. Retrieved from [source].*

- *McLuhan, M. (1964). Understanding Media: The Extensions of Man. McGraw-Hill.*

- *Morning Consult. (2019). Influencer Marketing: What Teens Think. Retrieved from [source].*

- *NIDA. (2019). Teen Drug Use and Trends. National Institute on Drug Abuse. Retrieved from [source].*

- *Patel, N. (2020). The Rise of Influencer Marketing: Trends and Implications. Retrieved from [source].*

- *Patchin, J. W., & Hinduja, S. (2018). Cyberbullying Among Adolescents: A Review of the Research. Journal of Adolescent Health. Retrieved from [source].*

- *Pew Research Center. (2018). Teens, Social Media & Technology 2018. Retrieved from [source].*

- *Sartre, J.-P. (1946). Existentialism is a Humanism. Yale University Press.*

- *Sensor Tower. (2020). TikTok and the Rise of Short-Form Video. Retrieved from [source].*

- *Stanford History Education Group. (2016). Evaluating Information: The Cornerstone of Civic Online Reasoning. Retrieved from [source].*

- *Twenge, J. M. (2017). iGen: Why Today's Super-Connected Kids Are Growing Up Less Rebellious, More Tolerant, Less Happy—and Completely Unprepared for Adulthood. Atria Books.*

- *Turkle, S. (2015). Reclaiming Conversation: The Power of Talk in a Digital Age. Penguin Books.*

3.   Morality in Freefall – A Comparative Analysis

As we venture into the heart of the moral maelstrom that is Gen Z, we're faced with a rather intriguing paradox: a generation that's more connected than ever yet seems to have lost its moral compass somewhere between Snapchat filters and TikTok dances. This chapter will dissect the shifting sands of morality, juxtapose Gen Z's ethical outlook with those of their predecessors, and explore how we arrived at this curious crossroads. Buckle up - it's going to be a bumpy ride through the turbulent terrain of modern morality.

3.1: The Moral Compass of Gen Z

Exploration of Gen Z's Moral Values Compared to Previous Generations

To understand Gen Z's moral landscape, we must first navigate the shifting terrain of their values. Unlike the rigid moral frameworks of previous generations, Gen Z's values are often described as fluid and context-dependent. This isn't to say they lack morals; rather, their moral compass operates on a different set of coordinates.

The traditional values of hard work, community, and discipline that characterized the Greatest Generation and Baby Boomers seem somewhat alien to a generation that prizes flexibility and self-expression. As philosopher Alain de Botton puts it, "Our moral judgments have become as varied as the choices available to us, and in this hyper-individualized world, morality is often seen as a matter of personal taste" (de Botton, 2012). For Gen Z, morality is less about adhering to universal principles and more about navigating a complex web of social norms and personal preferences.

Morality? Isn't That an App?

Let's face it - if you ask a Gen Zer what their moral compass looks like, they might just respond, "Is that an app?" In the age of rapid digital consumption, morality can sometimes seem as transient as the latest viral trend. The jokes may be amusing, but there's a kernel of truth in them. As sociologist Zygmunt Bauman observes, "In a liquid modern world, where everything is in flux, even moral principles seem to be constantly shifting" (Bauman, 2000). This fluidity can make it difficult to pin down what Gen Z truly values, leading to a moral landscape that's as unpredictable as a Twitter feed.

3.2: The Role of Parenting and Society

How Baby Boomers and Gen X Contributed to Shaping Gen Z

To understand how Gen Z's moral compass was forged, we need to look at the role of previous generations. Baby Boomers and Gen X, with their distinct parenting styles and societal contributions, have had a profound impact on shaping today's youth.

Baby Boomers, with their focus on traditional values and work ethics, laid the groundwork for the modern world. However, their emphasis on stability and conformity also contributed to the rise of Gen X's skepticism and individualism. Generation X, in turn, brought about a shift towards digitalization and a more fragmented society. As author and historian Neil Postman noted, "Each generation acts as a mirror reflecting the values and contradictions of its predecessors" (Postman, 1992). The shift from a more structured to a more fluid moral framework is a direct result of this intergenerational influence.

The Role of Media, Technology, and Changing Societal Norms

Media and technology have played pivotal roles in this moral transformation. The rise of social media has not only reshaped communication but also altered moral perceptions.

For example, the omnipresence of online platforms has amplified the visibility of various social issues, leading to a heightened awareness of social justice and ethical consumption.

However, this constant exposure has also contributed to the normalization of certain behaviors that might have been considered taboo in previous decades. The concept of "moral relativism," where right and wrong are viewed as subjective and context-dependent, has become more prevalent. As media scholar Marshall McLuhan famously remarked, "The medium is the message," suggesting that the platforms through which we communicate profoundly influence our moral perceptions (McLuhan, 1964). In a world where everyone is a publisher, it's no wonder that moral standards seem to be in constant flux.

3.3: Consequences of Moral Decline

The Impact on Relationships, Communities, and Societal Structures

The shifting moral landscape has had tangible effects on relationships, communities, and societal structures. The decline in traditional values has led to an erosion of trust and cohesion within communities. For instance, the rise of online interactions has transformed social relationships, often replacing face-to-face communication with virtual connections that can lack depth and authenticity. As psychologist Sherry Turkle points out, "Technology has given us the illusion of companionship without the demands of friendship" (Turkle, 2011).

In terms of societal structures, the erosion of traditional moral norms has impacted everything from workplace ethics to political discourse. The decline in shared values has led to increased polarization and fragmentation, making it more challenging to find common ground. According to political scientist Robert Putnam, "Social capital - the networks of trust and reciprocity that bind societies together - is in decline, and this has profound implications for the health of our communities" (Putnam, 2000).

Case Studies: From Cyber Scandals to the Erosion of Trust

To illustrate the consequences of this moral decline, let's examine a few case studies. The rise of cyber scandals, such as the Cambridge Analytica scandal, highlights the ethical lapses in the handling of personal data. This scandal exposed the manipulation of social media data for political gain, raising questions about privacy, consent, and accountability.

Another example is the erosion of trust in institutions, as seen in the decline of confidence in traditional media and *governmental bodies. According to a Gallup poll, trust in the media has reached historic lows, with only 41% of Americans expressing a great deal or fair amount of trust in the news media (Gallup, 2020). This decline in trust can be traced back to the increasing prevalence of misinformation and the blurring of lines between news and entertainment.*

These case studies illustrate the broader impact of moral decline on societal structures and relationships, offering a glimpse into the complex interplay between evolving values and the integrity of our institutions.

References

- *Bauman, Z. (2000). Liquid Modernity. Polity Press.*

- *de Botton, A. (2012). The News: A User's Manual. Pantheon Books.*

- *Gallup. (2020). Trust in Media. Retrieved from [source].*

- *McLuhan, M. (1964). Understanding Media: The Extensions of Man. McGraw-Hill.*

- *Postman, N. (1992). Technopoly: The Surrender of Culture to Technology. Knopf.*

- *Putnam, R. D. (2000). Bowling Alone: The Collapse and Revival of American Community. Simon & Schuster.*

- *Turkle, S. (2011). Alone Together: Why We Expect More from Technology and Less from Each Other. Basic Books.*

4. The Education Dilemma – Learning in the Age of Distraction

As we delve into the labyrinthine world of modern education, we encounter a curious paradox: a generation armed with unprecedented access to information, yet struggling with unprecedented levels of distraction. This chapter will explore the shifting paradigms of education in the age of digital abundance, examining how traditional learning is being upended, what the value of a degree is in an era dominated by TikTok, and how we can re-engage Gen Z in meaningful learning. Prepare for a journey through educational upheaval, with a dash of humor and melodrama to keep things lively.

4.1: The Decline of Formal Education

The Shift from Traditional Learning to YouTube Tutorials and Online Courses

In the not-so-distant past, formal education meant attending lectures, taking notes, and cramming for exams. Today, it means binge-watching YouTube tutorials, attending virtual workshops, and navigating the labyrinth of online courses. The traditional classroom is increasingly being replaced by digital platforms that offer bite-sized knowledge at the click of a button.

A 2019 report by the Pew Research Center found that 73% of teens use YouTube as a learning resource, with many preferring it to traditional classroom instruction (Pew Research Center, 2019). The appeal is clear: YouTube provides instant access to information and tutorials on virtually any topic, from algebra to astrophysics, often with a more engaging delivery than a dry textbook.

However, this shift has its drawbacks. The rise of online learning platforms has given birth to a new breed of educational shortcuts, such as diploma mills and exam cheating services. As education expert Richard Arum notes, "The proliferation of online credentials has blurred the lines between genuine learning and mere credentialism" (Arum, 2018). With the ease of access to both information and misinformation, distinguishing between quality education and educational fraud has become increasingly challenging.

The Rise of Exam Cheating and Diploma Mills

Exam cheating has become a cottage industry in the digital age. Whether through cheating apps, online forums, or pay-for-answers services, the temptation to cut corners is just a click away. A study by the International Center for Academic

Integrity found that 68% of students admit to cheating on at least one test during their academic career (International Center for Academic Integrity, 2018). This trend undermines the integrity of educational institutions and devalues genuine academic achievement.

Diploma mills, which offer degrees with little or no actual academic work, have also proliferated. According to a report by the Council for Higher Education Accreditation, these institutions often prey on individuals seeking to boost their credentials quickly and cheaply (CHEA, 2020). The ease with which degrees can be bought and sold has led to a devaluation of higher education and raised questions about the legitimacy of academic qualifications in the digital age.

4.2: The Value of a Degree in the TikTok Era

The Debate Over the Necessity of Higher Education

In a world where viral success stories and self-taught millionaires are common, the value of a traditional degree is increasingly questioned. The debate rages on: is higher education worth the time, money, and effort?

The tech industry, in particular, has seen several high-profile figures—like Steve Jobs and Mark Zuckerberg—who dropped out of college to pursue their entrepreneurial dreams. These success stories challenge the notion that a degree is a prerequisite for success. As economist Tyler Cowen argues, "The value of a college degree is diminishing, but the value of education—broadly conceived—is increasing" (Cowen, 2019).

Success Stories That Challenge Conventional Wisdom

Take, for example, the story of Alex Hormozi, an entrepreneur who built a multi-million-dollar business empire without a formal college degree. Hormozi's success underscores the notion that practical skills and entrepreneurial spirit can sometimes outweigh formal educational credentials. Similarly, Ben Silbermann, co-founder of Pinterest, dropped out of college to pursue his startup, which eventually became a household name.

These examples illustrate that while a degree may open doors, it is not necessarily the only path to success. However, they also highlight the importance of self-motivation, practical skills, and networking—elements that are not always emphasized in traditional education.

4.3: Solutions for Re-Engaging Gen Z in Learning

Innovative Education Models That Cater to Gen Z's Needs

To re-engage Gen Z, we must innovate. Traditional methods are increasingly out of sync with the learning preferences of today's youth. Educational models that emphasize interactive, project-based learning, and real-world applications are gaining traction.

One such model is the flipped classroom, where students review lecture material at home and engage in hands-on activities during class time. Research by the Bill & Melinda Gates Foundation shows that students in flipped classrooms often perform better and are more engaged than those in traditional settings (Gates Foundation, 2017). Another promising approach is gamification, which incorporates game-like elements into the learning process to increase motivation and engagement. As educational psychologist James Paul Gee notes, "Games are powerful learning tools because they engage students in a way that traditional methods do not" (Gee, 2003).

The Role of Educators, Parents, and Policymakers

Educators, parents, and policymakers all have roles to play in this educational renaissance. Educators must adapt their teaching strategies to meet the needs of a digital generation, incorporating technology and interactive methods into their curricula. Parents can support their children by fostering a positive attitude towards learning and encouraging curiosity and critical thinking.

Policymakers, meanwhile, need to address the structural challenges facing education, such as the rising cost of higher education and the need for more equitable access to quality resources. As education reform advocate Linda Darling-Hammond argues, "To truly transform education, we must address the underlying inequities and ensure that all students have access to high-quality learning opportunities" (Darling-Hammond, 2010).

References

- *Arum, R. (2018). The Underachieving College Student: What We Don't Know About College Education. University of Chicago Press.*

- *CHEA. (2020). The Rise of Diploma Mills: A Report. Council for Higher Education Accreditation. Retrieved from [source].*

- *Cowen, T. (2019). The Complacent Class: The Self-Defeating Quest for the American Dream. St. Martin's Press.*

- *Darling-Hammond, L. (2010). The Flat World and Education: How America's Commitment to Equity Will Determine Our Future. Teachers College Press.*

- *Gates Foundation. (2017). The Impact of Flipped Classrooms. Retrieved from [source].*

- *Gee, J. P. (2003). What Video Games Have to Teach Us About Learning and Literacy. Computers in the Schools, 20(3), 23-37.*

- *International Center for Academic Integrity. (2018). The State of Academic Integrity: A Report. Retrieved from [source].*

- *Pew Research Center. (2019). Teens, Social Media & Technology 2019. Retrieved from [source].*

5.   The Culture of Quick Fixes and Instant Gratification

In this age of one-click purchases and microwave meals, it's no surprise that the concept of patience is becoming increasingly foreign, especially for the Gen Z crowd. This chapter delves into the "fast everything" mentality, examining how the demand for speed is reshaping industries and what the psychological toll of instant gratification is on a generation that expects Rome not only to be built in a day but also with same-day shipping. It also proposes solutions - because yes, there's hope, even if it might take more than 30 seconds to explain.

5.1: The Instant Economy

How Gen Z's Demand for Speed Is Reshaping Industries

If the previous generations embraced hard work and long-term planning, Gen Z has mastered the art of efficiency - or, as some might argue, impatience. The "instant economy," driven by the demand for rapid service, has not only reshaped industries but also redefined how we view value and satisfaction. From fast fashion to fast food, convenience reigns supreme, but at what cost?

Fast fashion, for instance, churns out cheap, trendy clothes that can be worn today and discarded tomorrow. According to a report by the Ellen MacArthur Foundation, the average lifespan of a garment in the fast fashion industry is just seven wears (MacArthur, 2017). This need for constant newness and quick turnover, fueled largely by social media, is not only unsustainable but also responsible for the exploitation of labor and environmental degradation. As philosopher and social critic Byung-Chul Han notes, "In the age of acceleration, everything is fleeting, and the disposable culture has penetrated deep into our psyche" (Han, 2017).

This culture of speed extends beyond fashion into every aspect of life. Fast food chains, delivery services, and even entertainment industries cater to the "now" generation. As economist Daniel Susskind suggests, "The demand for speed and convenience in the digital era is reshaping labor markets and industries, leading to the gig economy where flexibility is prized over stability" (Susskind, 2020). However, in this pursuit of immediate gratification, we risk sacrificing quality, craftsmanship, and deeper satisfaction.

5.2: The Psychological Impact of Instant Gratification

Short-Term Thinking vs. Long-Term Planning

The psychology of instant gratification is not just about getting what we want faster; it's about how it shapes our thinking. Gen Z, raised in a digital environment where everything is at their fingertips, has developed a preference for short-term rewards over long-term gains. A study by psychologist Walter Mischel, famous for his marshmallow experiment, shows that the ability to delay gratification is linked to higher levels of success later in life (Mischel, 2014). However, in a world where social media likes provide instant validation, the capacity to wait and plan for the future is eroding.

This shift has significant consequences for mental health. According to a 2021 report by the American Psychological Association, Gen Z is experiencing higher levels of anxiety and depression compared to previous generations (APA, 2021). The pressure to constantly achieve and be "on" in the digital space has created a generation that is perpetually on edge. As clinical psychologist Jean Twenge puts it, "The immediacy of technology, combined with societal pressures, has created a perfect storm of mental health issues, where instant gratification becomes both a coping mechanism and a trap" (Twenge, 2018).

The consequences extend to broader societal behaviors. The pursuit of "easy success" has given rise to phenomena like *get-rich-quick schemes, online scams, and dubious self-help advice. As psychologist Barry Schwartz argues in The Paradox of Choice, "The overwhelming number of options and the drive for quick satisfaction can lead to decision fatigue, making individuals more anxious and less content" (Schwartz, 2004).*

The Rise of Anxiety, Depression, and Mental Health Issues

The constant barrage of digital stimuli, combined with the pursuit of instant gratification, has left many members of Gen Z struggling with mental health issues. The dopamine rush from a new notification or a like on social media provides a fleeting sense of joy, but it also contributes to long-term dissatisfaction and feelings of inadequacy. A study by Stanford University found that people who heavily rely on social media for validation are more prone to developing anxiety and depression (Stanford University, 2019).

Additionally, social media creates a space where comparison is rampant, and FOMO (Fear of Missing Out) intensifies the need for immediate action or gratification. Psychologist Jonathan Haidt, in his work on social media's effects on adolescents, writes, "The constant comparison to curated, idealized versions of others' lives exacerbates feelings of inadequacy and fosters an unhealthy need for immediate approval" (Haidt & Twenge, 2020).

5.3: Cultivating Patience and Resilience in a Fast World

Strategies for Promoting Delayed Gratification and Perseverance

While Gen Z's quick-fix mentality may be prevalent, it's not irreversible. Cultivating patience and resilience can be taught, but it requires deliberate effort from educators, parents, and individuals themselves. One key strategy is to reframe how we approach goals and rewards. Stanford psychologist Carol Dweck's research on the growth mindset shows that individuals who believe their abilities can develop through effort are more likely to persevere and achieve long-term success (Dweck, 2016). Shifting from a mindset of immediate success to one of gradual improvement is crucial in fostering resilience.

Another important approach is mindfulness and reflection, practices that have been proven to help individuals manage their impulses and reduce stress. Meditation apps like Headspace and Calm have gained popularity as tools for managing anxiety and promoting patience, even in the most fast-paced environments. As mindfulness expert Jon Kabat-Zinn notes, "Patience is not passive resignation; it is an active form of resilience that allows us to respond rather than react to life's challenges" (Kabat-Zinn, 1994).

Humor and Melodrama: "Rome Wasn't Built in a Day, But Gen Z Might Expect It To Be"

Let's face it - Rome wasn't built in a day, but if Gen Z had its way, it might expect it to be delivered via Amazon Prime, fully assembled, with free shipping. The joke, while humorous, touches on a serious reality: the unrealistic expectations created by living in a world of immediate solutions. The lesson here is simple: great things take time, whether it's building an empire or mastering a new skill. Perhaps we can all take a page from the Stoics, who believed in the power of patience and perseverance. After all, Marcus Aurelius didn't conquer the known world by binge-watching Netflix and ordering takeout.

References

- *American Psychological Association. (2021). Stress in America 2021: A National Mental Health Crisis. Retrieved from [source].*

- *Dweck, C. S. (2016). Mindset: The New Psychology of Success. Ballantine Books.*

- *Ellen MacArthur Foundation. (2017). A New Textiles Economy: Redesigning Fashion's Future. Retrieved from [source].*

- *Haidt, J., & Twenge, J. (2020). The Coddling of the American Mind: How Good Intentions and Bad Ideas Are Setting Up a Generation for Failure. Penguin Press.*

- *Han, B.-C. (2017). The Burnout Society. Stanford University Press.*

- *Kabat-Zinn, J. (1994). Wherever You Go, There You Are: Mindfulness Meditation in Everyday Life. Hyperion.*

- *Mischel, W. (2014). The Marshmallow Test: Understanding Self-Control and How To Master It. Little, Brown and Company.*

- *Schwartz, B. (2004). The Paradox of Choice: Why More Is Less. Harper Perennial.*

- *Susskind, D. (2020). A World Without Work: Technology, Automation, and How We Should Respond. Metropolitan Books.*

- *Stanford University. (2019). Social Media Use and Mental Health Among Adolescents: A Meta-Analysis. Retrieved from [source].*

- *Twenge, J. (2018). iGen: Why Today's Super-Connected Kids Are Growing Up Less Rebellious, More Tolerant, Less Happy—and Completely Unprepared for Adulthood. Atria Books.*

6. T -Savvy or Tech-Slave?

Ah, technology. That wondrous, miraculous force that connects us, empowers us, and sometimes... controls us. For Gen Z, the first true digital natives, the relationship with technology is a mixed bag - equal parts innovative and, let's be honest, a little terrifying. This chapter delves into the double-edged nature of tech-savviness. Is Gen Z leading the charge in a digital revolution, or are they unwittingly becoming tech's latest victims, enslaved to screens, addicted to online validation, and hacking their way into moral oblivion?

6.1: The Double-Edged Sword of Technology

The Benefits of Being Tech-Savvy: Innovation, Entrepreneurship, and Connectivity

Let's give credit where it's due: Gen Z is nothing short of impressive when it comes to navigating the digital world. They are natural-born innovators, having mastered coding, social media marketing, and content creation before they could legally vote. Tech-savviness has opened doors to unprecedented opportunities for entrepreneurship and self-expression. Take the case of young entrepreneurs like Ben Pasternak, who created his first tech startup at 15, or

Isabella Rose Taylor, a fashion designer who launched her own clothing line by age 13, leveraging social media to skyrocket her brand.

Economist Tyler Cowen suggests that "the ease of access to digital tools has democratized entrepreneurship in ways never before seen, making it possible for younger generations to enter the marketplace with minimal upfront investment" (Cowen, 2019). Indeed, platforms like Shopify, TikTok, and YouTube have become modern-day goldmines for those savvy enough to exploit them.

But let's not kid ourselves - along with these success stories come the overwhelming distractions and pitfalls of living in an always-connected world. The dopamine hit from a new notification can be as addictive as any drug. Studies show that Gen Z spends an average of 9 hours a day on their screens (Common Sense Media, 2019), often at the expense of their well-being, relationships, and even their ability to focus on the real world.

The Downside: Screen Addiction, Loss of Privacy, and Ethical Concerns

It's no secret that technology is addictive. According to psychologist Dr. Jean Twenge, author of iGen, "Gen Z is on the verge of a mental health crisis, with much of it tied to their constant exposure to social media and screen time" *(Twenge, 2018). Social media platforms are designed to keep users hooked, with algorithms that favor engagement over mental wellness. And while we applaud Gen Z for their technical prowess, there's a darker side to their digital lives.*

The loss of privacy is perhaps the most glaring issue. Data is the new oil, and companies are mining every digital footprint Gen Z leaves behind. From targeted ads to full-blown surveillance, privacy concerns loom large over the digital landscape. Philosopher Shoshana Zuboff calls this the "Age of Surveillance Capitalism," where our online behaviors are harvested, commodified, and sold to the highest bidder (Zuboff, 2019). But how concerned is Gen Z about their own data? According to a Pew Research Center report, only 26% of Gen Z users take active steps to protect their online privacy (Pew Research, 2021).

Ethical concerns extend beyond privacy to the very nature of online interactions. With misinformation, echo chambers, and trolling rampant on social media, digital platforms have become breeding grounds for some of society's ugliest behaviors. As Byung-Chul Han notes in In the Swarm, "In the digital world, the line between private and public collapses, creating a space where outrage and shallow connections thrive" (Han, 2017).

6.2: Hacking, Scams, and Cyber Crimes

The Rise of Digital Fraud, Hacking, and Online Scams

With great power comes great responsibility - or, in the case of Gen Z, great opportunity to delve into the darker corners of the web. From hacking to scamming, digital crime is on the rise, and Gen Z is no stranger to exploiting technological loopholes. In 2021 alone, cybercrime cost the global economy over $6 trillion (Cybersecurity Ventures, 2021), with a large portion of these crimes committed by tech-savvy youth.

Consider the rise of phishing scams, online fraud, and identity theft, all of which have skyrocketed in the past decade. A notorious example is the case of Graham Ivan Clark, a 17-year-old hacker who orchestrated one of the most high-profile social media breaches in history by hacking into Twitter accounts of celebrities like Elon Musk and Bill Gates, using them to promote a cryptocurrency scam (BBC, 2020). While such stories may seem like harmless teenage pranks, the damage caused is very real, both financially and ethically.

As sociologist Manuel Castells points out, "The digital world provides fertile ground for new forms of criminal activity, driven by the anonymity and global reach that the internet offers" (Castells, 2010). For Gen Z, who have grown up with the internet as their playground, the line between lawful and unlawful can often blur.

Case Studies and Anecdotes: How Gen Z Is Mastering the Dark Side of the Web

Beyond criminal activities, Gen Z has shown a knack for exploiting digital platforms in morally dubious ways. From creating fake social media profiles to gain followers to participating in viral "challenges" that border on dangerous, the dark side of digital literacy is real. In the words of philosopher Bernard Stiegler, "Technology, while expanding our capabilities, also diminishes our sense of responsibility" (Stiegler, 2011). The rapid pace of digital innovation outstrips the moral frameworks we have to guide its use, leaving Gen Z to navigate an ethical minefield.

6.3: Solutions for Responsible Tech Use

Digital Literacy, Ethics in Technology, and Cyber Education

All is not lost, however. The solution to Gen Z's complex relationship with technology lies in a twofold approach: education and regulation. Digital literacy programs that emphasize responsible use of technology, privacy protection, and ethical behavior are more critical than ever. As Dr. Larry Rosen, a leading expert on the psychology of technology, notes, "Tech education must go beyond coding skills - it must include critical thinking about technology's role in society and personal well-being" (Rosen, 2016).

Furthermore, cyber education needs to start early, equipping young users with the tools to navigate the web safely and ethically. Initiatives like Common Sense Media's digital literacy curriculum are paving the way, teaching young people about privacy, cyberbullying, and misinformation. In parallel, tech companies must also step up, implementing stricter regulations and improving transparency in how data is collected and used.

The Role of Parents, Educators, and Tech Companies

Parents and educators play a crucial role in guiding Gen Z toward healthier tech habits. Limiting screen time, promoting offline activities, and fostering open discussions about the dangers of the digital world are essential. As economist Sherry Turkle argues in Reclaiming Conversation, "The antidote to digital overindulgence is fostering genuine, face-to-face human interaction" (Turkle, 2015). Without these human connections, Gen Z risks losing sight of the bigger picture - of real relationships, real values, and real life.

Tech companies, too, hold a large share of responsibility. With ethical tech design, companies can create platforms that prioritize mental well-being and responsible behavior. Social media giants like Instagram and Twitter have already begun implementing features to curb addiction and cyberbullying, but more work is needed. As Zuboff notes, "The future of technology must be one that prioritizes human flourishing over profit" (Zuboff, 2019).

References

- *BBC. (2020). "Twitter hack: Florida teenager 'mastermind' pleads guilty." Retrieved from [source].*

- *Castells, M. (2010). The Rise of the Network Society. Wiley-Blackwell.*

- *Common Sense Media. (2019). The Common Sense Census: Media Use by Tweens and Teens. Retrieved from [source].*

- *Cowen, T. (2019). Big Business: A Love Letter to an American Anti-Hero. St. Martin's Press.*

- *Cybersecurity Ventures. (2021). 2021 Official Annual Cybercrime Report. Retrieved from [source].*

- *Han, B.-C. (2017). In the Swarm: Digital Prospects. MIT Press.*

- *Pew Research Center. (2021). Gen Z, Millennials Stand Out for Climate Change Activism, Social Media Engagement with Issue. Retrieved from [source].*

- *Rosen, L. (2016). The Distracted Mind: Ancient Brains in a High-Tech World. MIT Press.*

- *Stiegler, B. (2011). The Decadence of Industrial Democracies. Polity Press.*

- *Turkle, S. (2015). Reclaiming Conversation: The Power of Talk in a Digital Age. Penguin Press.*

- *Twenge, J. (2018). iGen: Why Today's Super-Connected Kids Are Growing Up Less Rebellious, More Tolerant, Less Happy—and Completely Unprepared for Adulthood. Atria Books.*

- *Zuboff, S. (2019). The Age of Surveillance Capitalism: The Fight for a Human Future at the New Frontier of Power. PublicAffairs.*

7. The Global Impact of the Gen Z Mindset

As Gen Z comes of age, their influence on the global stage is becoming undeniable. From championing social causes to reshaping economies and redefining governance, they are determined to make their mark - whether the world is ready for it or not. In this chapter, we'll explore how the unique blend of Gen Z's values, ideals, and behaviors is shaking up the status quo in areas ranging from activism to the economy and beyond. Will they save the world or simply tweet about it? That's the trillion-dollar question.

7.1: Social Justice Warriors or Keyboard Warriors?

Gen Z's Role in Global Movements: Climate Change, Equality, and Human Rights

Give Gen Z a hashtag, and they'll turn it into a global movement. Whether it's #BlackLivesMatter, #MeToo, or #FridaysForFuture, this generation has proven itself adept at using social media to rally people around the world. Climate change, gender equality, and human rights are front and center for Gen Z, whose members have taken up the mantle of activism from their predecessors but with a distinctly digital twist.

Take, for instance, Greta Thunberg, the Swedish environmental activist who, at just 16, ignited a global youth climate strike. Thunberg's unapologetic stance - "I want you to panic" (Thunberg, 2019) - has inspired millions of young people to take to the streets (and their Instagram stories) to demand action on climate change. Economist Jeffrey Sachs argues that "the mobilization of Gen Z around climate change is one of the most powerful movements of our time" (Sachs, 2020).

But is this activism as deep as it appears, or is it just a case of keyboard warriors using social justice as a trendy backdrop for their TikToks? Psychologist Dr. Sherry Turkle raises an interesting point, stating that "while Gen Z is highly engaged online, there is a danger that this activism lacks depth when it is primarily expressed through tweets and likes" (Turkle, 2015). This brings us to the phenomenon of **slacktivism***, where posting about an issue feels like doing something, but the real-world impact is minimal. It's activism light, if you will, with all the moral virtue and none of the effort.*

The Fine Line Between Activism and Slacktivism

It's easy to see how Gen Z's activism could veer into performative territory. With the rise of influencer culture, many movements become less about the cause and more about the aesthetics of protest. Wearing a "Save the Earth" T-shirt is cool, but how many of those shirts are sustainably made? Philosopher Slavoj Žižek argues that "we live in an era where activism is often commodified, and social causes are turned into products to be consumed rather than movements to change society" (Žižek, 2014).

And yet, slacktivism shouldn't be dismissed entirely. Digital platforms allow Gen Z to spread awareness on a global scale, bringing critical issues to the forefront. While not everyone may attend a protest or lobby their government, the sheer volume of online support for causes like Black Lives Matter has forced both policymakers and corporations to take notice. As sociologist Zeynep Tufekci notes, "Online activism may be criticized for its superficiality, but it also has the power to spark significant offline change" (Tufekci, 2017).

7.2: The Economic Impact

How Gen Z's Spending Habits and Career Choices Are Reshaping Economies

It's no secret that Gen Z is breaking the mold when it comes to spending and career preferences. Traditional consumer patterns? Out the window. This generation favors *experiences over possessions, values sustainability, and demands that brands align with their ethical standards. A report by McKinsey reveals that "Gen Z consumers are driving the shift toward more ethical consumption, with 72% of them willing to pay extra for sustainable products" (McKinsey, 2021).*

But it's not just their spending habits that are shaking things up—Gen Z's approach to work is rewriting the rules of the global economy. Traditional 9-to-5 jobs? No, thank you. This generation prefers flexibility, remote work, and side hustles. According to economist Richard Florida, the rise of the gig economy and freelance work is largely driven by younger workers who "prioritize work-life balance and personal fulfillment over job security" (Florida, 2018).

The Rise of Gig Work, Remote Jobs, and the Decline of Traditional Industries

The shift toward gig work and freelancing has given birth to what some call the "Youpreneur" generationindividuals who leverage platforms like Etsy, Fiverr, and Patreon - to turn hobbies into income streams. This trend has been accelerated by the COVID-19 pandemic, which normalized remote work and led many to reconsider the necessity of physical offices altogether.

But with this rise in freelancing comes new challenges, especially regarding job security and benefits. "The gig economy offers freedom," says economist Guy Standing, "but it also comes with the risks of precarity and exploitation" (Standing, 2016). Gen Z workers may enjoy their autonomy now, but what happens when they face the long-term consequences of unstable income and lack of health benefits?

The economic impact of Gen Z also extends to the industries they are abandoning. Take, for instance, brick-and-mortar retail, which is in steady decline as Gen Z turns to e-commerce for nearly all their shopping needs. Economist Daniel Bell posits that "we are witnessing a structural shift in the economy, where industries reliant on in-person interactions are giving way to digital-first models" (Bell, 2021). The ripple effects are vast, impacting not just retailers but real estate, manufacturing, and service industries.

7.3: The Future of Governance and Leadership

How Gen Z's Values May Influence Future Political and Social Systems

Gen Z is coming, and they're bringing their values with them. From an emphasis on social justice to demands for transparency, this generation will soon hold the reins of power. But what will their leadership look like? Will they *usher in a new age of inclusivity and equality, or will their idealism crumble under the weight of real-world governance?*

Political scientist Francis Fukuyama suggests that "Gen Z's deep mistrust of institutions, combined with their demand for systemic change, will lead to significant political shifts in the coming decades" (Fukuyama, 2019). Already, Gen Z is influencing politics, with many advocating for progressive policies on climate change, healthcare, and social equality. However, their skepticism toward traditional political parties may also pave the way for more decentralized forms of governance, such as direct democracy or blockchain-based voting systems.

Potential Scenarios: From Utopia to Dystopia

But the future isn't all sunshine and rainbows. Some philosophers, like Yuval Noah Harari, warn that "while Gen Z's reliance on technology offers opportunities for innovation, it also opens the door to dystopian outcomes, where tech monopolies and surveillance states dominate the political landscape" (Harari, 2018). In other words, the same tools that Gen Z uses to advocate for change could easily be weaponized by authoritarian regimes to suppress dissent.

In a more optimistic scenario, Gen Z's commitment to diversity, inclusion, and sustainability could lead to more equitable and just societies. As political theorist John Rawls famously stated, "A just society is one in which the least advantaged are empowered to thrive" (Rawls, 1971). With their focus on human rights and social justice, Gen Z could be the generation that brings this vision to life.

However, the path to utopia is fraught with challenges. In the words of cultural critic Mark Fisher, "The future is always contested, and the forces of neoliberalism and reactionary politics will not go quietly" (Fisher, 2009). The key question is whether Gen Z will be able to navigate the complexities of leadership while staying true to their ideals—or whether they will fall prey to the same forces of corruption and power that have derailed generations before them.

References

- *Bell, D. (2021). The Coming of Post-Industrial Society. Basic Books.*

- *Fisher, M. (2009). Capitalist Realism: Is There No Alternative? Zero Books.*

- *Florida, R. (2018). The Rise of the Creative Class. Basic Books.*

- *Fukuyama, F. (2019). Identity: The Demand for Dignity and the Politics of Resentment. Farrar, Straus, and Giroux.*

- *Harari, Y. N. (2018). 21 Lessons for the 21st Century. Spiegel & Grau.*

- *McKinsey & Company. (2021). The Gen Z Consumer Report. Retrieved from [source].*

- *Sachs, J. (2020). The Age of Sustainable Development. Columbia University Press.*

- *Standing, G. (2016). The Precariat: The New Dangerous Class. Bloomsbury Academic.*

- *Thunberg, G. (2019). Speech at the World Economic Forum in Davos. Retrieved from [source].*

8. Reclaiming the Future - Solutions and Hope

Ah, the grand finale. After wading through the chaos of digital addiction, slacktivism, and the gig economy, we arrive at the part where we – hopefully - figure out how to fix things. Don't worry; we've saved the melodrama for last. In this chapter, we'll explore real solutions for bridging generational divides, restoring values, and, yes, even reclaiming the future. Let's face it: if we don't address these issues now, we might find ourselves in a dystopia where the robots are our bosses and the only form of activism left is liking memes.

8.1: Bridging the Generational Gap

Encouraging Dialogue and Understanding Between Generations

Let's set the scene: you're at a family dinner. Grandpa is lecturing everyone about how "kids these days" can't survive without their phones, while your younger cousin is TikToking her latest dance routine. Tensions rise, eye-rolls ensue, and before you know it, everyone is texting under the table. Sound familiar? Bridging the generational gap is tough, but it's also essential if we want to move forward as a society.

The truth is, generations have always struggled to understand each other. Baby Boomers don't get Millennials, Millennials don't get Gen Z, and Gen Z? Well, they're just trying to survive the apocalypse they feel they've been handed. Philosopher Friedrich Nietzsche once remarked, "One generation misjudges the other; that is how the world comes to ruin" (Nietzsche, 1888). But, of course, he didn't have to deal with Wi-Fi passwords and Snapstreaks, so we'll cut him some slack.

How to Talk to a Gen Z Without Losing Your Mind

*Let's get real—talking to Gen Z can sometimes feel like trying to decode the Rosetta Stone. Between the acronyms (BRB, FOMO, SMH) and the existential crises ("What's the point of capitalism anyway?"), older generations often find themselves on the verge of a meltdown. But here's the thing: **communication is key**. We can't solve anything if we're talking past each other.*

Psychologist Dr. Jean Twenge, known for her work on generational differences, explains that "Gen Z is the most anxious generation yet, largely due to their immersion in technology and social media" (Twenge, 2017). To talk to them without losing your mind, you need to meet them where they are - online, empathetic, and open to understanding their worldview. Humor helps, too. As educator John Dewey once said, "Laughter relieves us of superfluous energy, which, if it remained unused, might become negative, that is, poisonous, and have a detrimental effect on our health" (Dewey, 1916). So, go ahead - crack a joke about TikTok. You'll be surprised at how quickly it can lighten the mood.

8.2: Restoring Values and Morality

Strategies for Reintroducing Ethical and Moral Education

In a world where moral compasses seem as rare as payphones, how do we restore values and ethics? The answer, dear reader, lies in education - not just in schools, but at home and in communities. "The moral education of the younger generation is not merely a task for the schools; it is a collective endeavor for families, religious institutions, and civil society," writes sociologist Robert Putnam (Putnam, 2015).

You may have heard the old adage, "It takes a village to raise a child." Well, in 2024, it takes a global village - and by that, I mean parents, teachers, Instagram influencers, and AI chatbots. The real challenge is balancing traditional values with the rapid technological advancements of today's world. Philosopher Alasdair MacIntyre, in his classic work After Virtue, argued that "moral education must be rooted in the community, where individuals are shaped by shared practices and traditions" (MacIntyre, 1981). This holds true now more than ever.

*But let's be honest: getting Gen Z to care about anything that isn't happening on their phones is tricky. That's where schools and families come in, and not just through lectures about the "good old days." What's needed is **engagement** - moral lessons that relate to the world Gen Z is living in now. An ethics class that tackles issues like data privacy, cyberbullying, and climate justice is far more likely to stick than one that spends an hour pontificating about Plato's Republic.*

The Role of Families, Schools, and Communities in Fostering Values

It's not enough to hope that kids will somehow pick up ethical behavior through osmosis. Families must take an active role in discussing right and wrong, while schools should incorporate moral philosophy into their curriculums. And communities? Well, they need to model the behavior they want to see. "Children learn more from what you are than what you teach," famously said psychologist Carl Jung (Jung, 1953). If we want to restore a sense of morality, the change has to start with us.

And let's not forget the power of stories. Anthropologist Joseph Campbell argues that myths and narratives have always been key tools for teaching values (Campbell, 1949). In today's world, these stories may come in the form of YouTube videos or Netflix series, but the impact is the same. The moral of the story is simple: if we want to restore values, we need to make them relevant to the lives Gen Z is living today.

8.3: The Road Ahead – Building a Better Tomorrow

Visionary Ideas for a Future Where Gen Z Contributes Positively to Society

Ah, the future - bright, uncertain, and full of potential. If Gen Z is going to reclaim it, they'll need to focus on solutions that build a better tomorrow for everyone. Luckily, despite all the doom and gloom, this generation is full of visionaries. Entrepreneurial, socially conscious, and tech-savvy, they have the tools to create meaningful change if they can avoid getting trapped in the endless scroll of distractions.

According to education expert Sir Ken Robinson, "The future belongs to the creatives and problem-solvers. Gen Z must be empowered to think critically and innovate if we are to solve the great challenges ahead" (Robinson, 2015). So, what are the visionary ideas that can propel Gen Z toward a brighter future?

*First and foremost, **mentorship** is crucial. Gen Z needs guidance from those who've walked the path before them - without being condescending, of course. Sociologist Erik Erikson emphasizes the importance of intergenerational mentorship, noting that "each generation must learn from its predecessors, or it risks making the same mistakes" (Erikson, 1968). Mentorship can provide Gen Z with the wisdom they need to navigate an increasingly complex world, while still allowing them the freedom to innovate and disrupt.*

The Importance of Mentorship, Education, and Responsible Technology Use

Education, particularly in the form of digital literacy, will be the linchpin for Gen Z's success. In an age where information is abundant but wisdom is scarce, teaching young people how to critically evaluate sources, protect their privacy, and use technology responsibly is more important than ever. As media scholar Neil Postman famously said, "Technology always comes at a price. It giveth, and it taketh away" (Postman, 1993). Gen Z must learn to harness the benefits of technology while mitigating its risks.

Finally, the road ahead must include a serious reckoning with the environmental crisis. Gen Z is already leading the charge, but they'll need all the help they can get to tackle climate change, biodiversity loss, and environmental degradation. As economist Kate Raworth suggests, "We must move beyond growth as the sole measure of progress and instead focus on creating a regenerative economy that works within the planet's boundaries" (Raworth, 2017). Gen Z is up to the task, but they'll need strong partnerships with older generations, businesses, and governments to make it happen.

Conclusion: Reclaiming the Future

So, what have we learned? Gen Z may be facing an uphill battle, but with the right tools - mentorship, moral education, and responsible tech use - they can build a future that benefits us all. As we navigate this generational transition, we must remember that understanding, dialogue, and shared responsibility are key. After all, as philosopher Simone de Beauvoir once said, "The future is not some place we are going to, but one we are creating" (de Beauvoir, 1949).

References

- *Campbell, J. (1949). The Hero with a Thousand Faces. Princeton University Press.*

- *Dewey, J. (1916). Democracy and Education. Macmillan.*

- *Erikson, E. H. (1968). Identity: Youth and Crisis. W.W. Norton & Company.*

- *Jung, C. G. (1953). Psychological Reflections. Bollingen Series.*

- *MacIntyre, A. (1981). After Virtue: A Study in Moral Theory. University of Notre Dame Press.*

- *Nietzsche, F. (1888). Twilight of the Idols. Penguin Classics.*

- *Postman, N. (1993). Technopoly: The Surrender of Culture to Technology. Vintage.*

- *Putnam, R. D. (2015). Our Kids: The American Dream in Crisis. Simon & Schuster.*

The Gen Z Apocalypse - Or a New Beginning?

Well, here we are - the grand finale of the Gen Z Apocalypse. After dissecting the rise of screen addictions, slacktivism, cybercrime, and the ever-evolving gig economy, it's time to reflect. Is this really the end of days, or have we simply reached the intermission? Spoiler alert: the story doesn't end here.

Gen Z, for all its quirks, is not a generation doomed to dystopia. Quite the opposite. Beneath the memes and the TikTok dances lies a group of individuals with more potential than we've seen in generations. But, as we've explored, it's a double-edged sword - a fine line between brilliance and chaos, innovation and destruction. Let's dive into some reflections, a call to action, and, of course, end on a hopeful note. After all, we're not that cynical.

Reflections: Summarizing the Key Points and Highlighting the Urgency

First, let's recap our rollercoaster ride through the landscape of Gen Z:

- *__Technology__: The ultimate double-edged sword, capable of both empowering entrepreneurship and triggering addiction. Remember the time when we* *marveled at how Gen Z could code an app in their sleep? Now, we're just trying to pry them away from 14 hours of screen time a day (Twenge, 2017).*

- ***Activism:** The passionate energy of Gen Z is undeniable. They care deeply about climate change, equality, and social justice, but there's also the rise of "slacktivism" where changing a profile picture becomes mistaken for true activism (Gladwell, 2010).*

- ***Economics:** As Gen Z reshapes the job market, freelancing and gig work have become the new normal, but this shift has come with economic instability. The challenge is finding a way to make this gig economy sustainable for future generations (Friedman, 2020).*

- ***Moral Values:** As philosopher Alasdair MacIntyre warned, the erosion of shared moral frameworks leaves us floating in a sea of relativism (MacIntyre, 1981). For Gen Z, the task is finding a way to rebuild a sense of ethics in a hyper-digital, individualistic world.*

The urgency of addressing these issues cannot be overstated. The world is rapidly changing, and Gen Z is at the forefront. Yet, they need guidance, mentorship, and strong moral compasses to navigate this chaotic era. Otherwise, we risk letting this so-called "apocalypse" spiral out of control.

Call to Action: Meaningful Dialogue and Practical Steps

*Let's not just stand around lamenting the demise of civilization as we know it. It's time for some action. The issues we've discussed in this book aren't abstract—they're very real, and they're impacting us right now. We need intergenerational dialogue. Not the kind where Millennials and Boomers grumble about avocado toast and "entitlement," but the kind where we sit down and figure out how to move forward **together**.*

Economist and social theorist Amartya Sen put it perfectly: "No generation can solve the problems of the world in isolation. It requires the wisdom of the past, the energy of the present, and the hope of the future" (Sen, 1999). Gen Z has that energy in spades, but they need the wisdom of older generations to channel it effectively.

***Practical steps?** Here's what we need:*

- ***Mentorship**: Let's create spaces where older generations can mentor Gen Z, sharing knowledge without condescension. As sociologist Erik Erikson emphasized, the transfer of knowledge between generations is essential for societal stability (Erikson, 1968).*

- ***Digital Literacy and Ethics****: Schools need to teach not just how to use technology but how to use it responsibly. Let's foster critical thinking about online privacy, digital identity, and ethics in tech (Postman, 1993).*

- ***Community Building****: Let's restore the values of community and shared responsibility. It's time to start bridging the digital divide—no, not the one about broadband access, but the emotional and moral divide that's widened in our hyper-individualistic world (Putnam, 2000).*

*Sure, Gen Z can be overwhelming. Their slang is baffling, their attention span rivals that of a goldfish, and they seem more interested in being "woke" than awake. But let's not forget one thing: **they're us, just in a more caffeinated, digitally-saturated form**. Every generation has had its crisis, and every generation has found a way to rise above it.*

As historian Yuval Noah Harari humorously notes, "History is often shaped by the young and foolish—those who don't know what's impossible tend to achieve it" (Harari, 2014). Gen Z may be young, but they are far from foolish. They are ambitious, tech-savvy, and fiercely idealistic. With the right guidance, they could be the generation that solves climate change, ends systemic inequality, and creates a more compassionate global society.

Optimism? Absolutely. The so-called Gen Z "apocalypse" is not the end; it's a beginning. Gen Z has the tools and the passion to build a future where technology works for us, not against us, where activism leads to real change, and where morality and ethics are rediscovered, not lost in the noise.

So, let's not give up hope. If anything, we should be excited to see where Gen Z takes us. As Dr. Seuss wisely said, "Oh, the places you'll go!" We may be standing on the edge of an apocalypse, but with a little help, Gen Z might just lead us to a better world.

References

- Erikson, E. H. (1968). Identity: Youth and Crisis. W.W. Norton & Company.

- Friedman, T. L. (2020). Thank You for Being Late: An Optimist's Guide to Thriving in the Age of Accelerations. Picador.

- Gladwell, M. (2010). Small Change: Why the Revolution Will Not Be Tweeted. The New Yorker.

- *Harari, Y. N. (2014). Sapiens: A Brief History of Humankind. Harper.*

- *MacIntyre, A. (1981). After Virtue: A Study in Moral Theory. University of Notre Dame Press.*

- *Postman, N. (1993). Technopoly: The Surrender of Culture to Technology. Vintage.*

- *Putnam, R. D. (2000). Bowling Alone: The Collapse and Revival of American Community. Simon & Schuster.*

- *Sen, A. (1999). Development as Freedom. Oxford University Press.*

- *Twenge, J. M. (2017). iGen: Why Today's Super-Connected Kids Are Growing Up Less Rebellious, More Tolerant, Less Happy--and Completely Unprepared for Adulthood. Atria Books.*

- *Raworth, K. (2017). Doughnut Economics: Seven Ways to Think Like a 21st-Century Economist. Chelsea Green Publishing.*

- *Robinson, K. (2015). Creative Schools: The Grassroots Revolution That's Transforming Education. Viking.*

- *Twenge, J. M. (2017). iGen: Why Today's Super-Connected Kids Are Growing Up Less Rebellious, More Tolerant, Less Happy—and Completely Unprepared for Adulthood. Atria Books.*

- *de Beauvoir, S. (1949). The Second Sex. Vintage Books.*

About the Author

Grayson Whitlock, *the self-proclaimed "reluctant professor of Gen Z absurdities" and your go-to guide through the delightful chaos that is modern society. Grayson is a man of many talents—writer, philosopher, occasional stand-up comedian (by accident), and the world's most frustrated mentor to the digital generation. Armed with an uncanny ability to blend humor with hard-hitting truths, Grayson has made it his mission to dissect the trials and tribulations of today's youth—particularly the wild bunch known as Generation Z.*

Growing up, Grayson never imagined he'd one day be an expert on TikTok trends or spend sleepless nights wondering why the youth prefer filters over face-to-face conversations. But here we are, and Grayson has turned his bewilderment into something productive, writing books that are equal parts hilarious and soul-searching.

Interesting Story:

Legend has it that Grayson once tried to teach a group of Gen Zers the value of patience by forcing them to watch a documentary—on VHS. The look of horror on their faces is something Grayson will carry with him for the rest of his days. And, yes, he still owns a VCR. "How else do you teach people what waiting feels like?" he'll quip.

Instructing Side:

Behind the humor and well-placed jokes, Grayson is deeply committed to guiding people—especially parents and educators—on how to bridge the ever-widening gap between generations. He writes with both empathy and urgency, balancing wit with wisdom in a way that keeps readers engaged but also makes them think, reflect, and (hopefully) act. He's the kind of writer who will make you laugh one minute and then drop a truth bomb so profound that you'll put the book down and stare at the ceiling for a few minutes, just to process it.

Why Take Him Seriously?

Because for all the jokes, Grayson is asking the right questions and providing solutions for real-world problems. He may joke about Gen Z turning Rome into an app or how morality is now a forgotten hashtag, but his insights into social and moral decay are sharp, thoughtful, and backed by serious research. He has a knack for making you laugh at the ridiculousness of the world, while also giving you the tools to make it better.

In short, Grayson Whitlock is the voice you didn't know you needed—a charming balance of humor, intellect, and practical advice for navigating the apocalypse... or, as he calls it, "a Tuesday with Gen Z."

Notes

Notes

Notes

Notes

www.ingramcontent.com/pod-product-compliance
Lightning Source LLC
LaVergne TN
LVHW051712050326
832903LV00032B/4155